How ~~to Survive in~~ the

Himalayas

Simon Chapman

Badger Publishing Limited
Oldmedow Road,
Hardwick Industrial Estate,
King's Lynn PE30 4JJ
Telephone: 01438 791037

www.badgerlearning.co.uk

2 4 6 8 10 9 7 5 3 1

How to Trek the Himalayas ISBN 978-1-78464-026-2

Publisher: Susan Ross
Senior Editor: Danny Pearson
Publishing Assistant: Claire Morgan
Designer: Fiona Grant
Series Consultant: Dee Reid

Photos: Cover: Christian Kober/Robert Hardi/REX
Page 6: Simon Chapman
Page 7: Simon Chapman
Page 8: Simon Chapman
Page 9: Simon Chapman
Page 10: Simon Chapman
Page 11: National Geographic/Getty Images
Page 12: © Stefano Politi Markovina/Alamy
Page 13: AFP/Getty Images
Page 14: © Suzanne Long/Alamy
Page 15: Simon Chapman
Page 17: Image Broker/REX
Page 18: © Design Pics Inc./Alamy
Page 19: Simon Chapman
Page 20: Simon Chapman
Page 21: © Craig Lovell/Eagle Visions Photography/Alamy
Page 22: © Dmitry Rukhlenko – Photos of India/Alamy
Page 23: © LatitudeStock/Alamy
Page 24: Peter Barritt/Robert Harding/REX
Page 25: © National Geographic Image Collection/Alamy
Page 26: Peter Barritt/Robert Harding/REX
Page 27: © Craig Lovell/Eagle Visions Photography/Alamy
Page 28: Pacific Press Service/REX
Page 30: Simon Chapman

Attempts to contact all copyright holders have been made.
If any omitted would care to contact Badger Learning, we will be happy to make appropriate arrangements.

How to Trek the Himalayas

Contents

Badger

Vocabulary

altitude	landslide
crampons	leech
crystals	mountain
herbivore	oxygen

You are planning a trek through the Himalayan mountains in Nepal.

You will be walking up narrow paths and down steep valleys. You will cross icy cold streams.

Keep on the look out! You might come across a Yeti!

1. Preparation

The Himalayan mountain range runs across Pakistan and India through Nepal, all the way to Western China.

The world's ten highest peaks are here, including Mount Everest, which is nearly six miles high and the biggest mountain of them all.

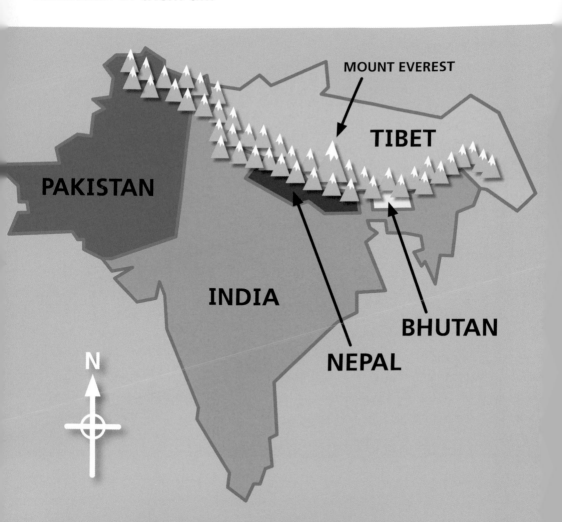

For hundreds of years people have been crossing the Himalayas, taking tea to India or trekking to holy mountains.

You will use the ancient trails to travel deep into the mountain range.

You can hire a jeep and driver to get you to the end of the road, but then you'll have to walk the rest of the way.

What should you take with you?

Food
Take rice and pasta, which give you energy but are not too heavy to carry.

Clothes
Your trek will start in hot, damp forests but, as the trail climbs higher, the weather gets colder.

You will need a waterproof coat and warm layers to keep out the cold. You will need good hiking boots.

You're going to be doing a lot of walking.

You will need to hire pack horses to carry your supplies.

2. River crossing

Take care as you walk up the paths on the lower slopes of the mountain.

The paths are very muddy and you might slip. There are many small streams and some larger rivers you will have to cross. These rivers are fast-flowing and freezing cold.

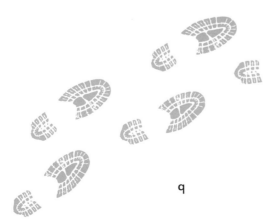

In some places in the Himalayas there are zip wires across rivers. This is a really fast way to cross the river, but watch you don't fall off the wire into the swirling waters below!

Tips for crossing rivers

1. Use a walking stick or pole to give you extra balance.

2. Walk facing the flow of the water

3. Lean forwards towards your pole.

4. Put old socks over your boots. This will give you a better grip on wet rocks than walking in your boots.

5. Make sure you can get your backpack off easily if you fall in. It's better to lose your belongings than your life!

6. If you do fall in, make sure your feet are facing downstream. That way, you can kick yourself away from any rocks that you might crash into.

3. Landslide

Watch out!

Sometimes whole sections of the path have been swept away by landslides.

Now you have no path to follow. In front of you are just mud and rocks.

You have to climb over the mud and rocks to find the path again.

Crossing the landslide is risky. The mud is slippery and one wrong move will make it slide again, taking you down with it.

Tie one end of a rope to a tree before you cross. The first person across should tie the other end of the rope to a rock for the other people to hold onto as they cross the landslide.

4. Animals of the Himalayas

Watch out for leeches. These are attracted to your body heat. They climb onto you and wriggle inside your clothes to suck your blood.

Ripping a leech off leaves a bleeding wound.

How to remove a leech

Find the sucker at the small end of the leech.

Put your finger on your skin next to the sucker.

Slide your finger towards the wound
where the leech is feeding.

Use your fingernail, to push the sucker
sideways away from your skin.

Once you have moved the sucker away from your
skin, quickly pull away the fat end of the leech.

Then try flicking the leech away.

Take care! As you work to remove the leech,
it will try to suck onto your skin again.

Look out for these animals on your trek:

Red panda

Like the giant panda, the red panda feeds on bamboo.
It is endangered as the forests where it lives are being
destroyed.

Snow leopard

These leopards have long, thick fur and pale green eyes. They use their long tails to help them balance on the rocky slopes of the mountains.

Snub-nosed monkey

These monkeys have thick fur and tiny noses.

WOW! facts

Snub-nosed monkeys live at a higher altitude than any other monkey. They are used to cold temperatures.

Yaks

The only farm animals that do well this high up the mountain are yaks.

Yaks are like cows, but they have long fur and larger lungs so they can live at high altitudes.

You might see them grazing on the mountain sides.

Yak facts

- The yak is a herbivore (that is, it eats grass and flowers).
- It has four stomachs.
- After it has swallowed its food it brings it up again and chews it a bit more!
- It has horns, which it uses to break through snow in order to get the plants that are buried beneath it.

You might be offered a cup of tea made with yak butter instead of milk! Yuk!

5. Thin air and blinding light

As you climb higher, leaving the forest behind, you will feel the air getting colder.

You will also find it harder to breathe. Why? Because you are several thousand metres above sea level and there is less oxygen in the air.

This means you will have to walk slower and rest more often.

Altitude sickness

You might also get headaches and find it difficult to get to sleep at night.

This is altitude sickness. Most people get over this in a few days but, if the headaches get really bad, then you must get back down to a lower level quickly. People can die of altitude sickness.

Sun and snow

As you trek higher up the mountain you reach the first patches of snow.

The wind is strong up here but so is the sun. You will need to wear a hat and put on lots of sunscreen.

It's also a good idea to wear sunglasses. If possible, find sunglasses that have side pieces.

These will be useful when you're crossing the snow fields as they stop tiny ice crystals blowing across your eyes.

The bright sun shining on the white snow and the strong wind will make your eyes sting and water a lot.

It will feel like you have got grit in your eyes and they will still sting even when you close them. Take care, this can lead to 'snow blindness'.

What to do if you get snow blindness:
- Get out of the sun as quickly as you can.
- Stay inside your tent.
- Put a cool, damp cloth on your eyes.

It may take three days for your eyes to get better.

6. The roof of the world

Now you are looking up at the snowy peaks all around you. Those peaks above you are huge. That's why the Himalayas are sometimes called 'the roof of the world'.

So far you have managed your trek with strong boots and a walking pole. If you want to climb higher up the mountain you will need proper climbing gear.

Climbing gear

- ice axes

- crampons
(Spikes to put on your boots
to help them grip the ice)

- ropes

- a safety helmet

- oxygen bottles to breathe from

Climbing Everest is very
dangerous. Over 250 climbers
have died trying to climb it.

Trekking in the Himalayas is not for wimps!

You need to be fit and strong.

If you don't slip into an icy river or get leeches or snow blindness you could have the holiday of a lifetime!

Questions

Which countries do the Himalayas cover? *(page 5)*

What are zip wires used for? *(page 10)*

How do you cross a landslide? *(page 14)*

How do leeches find you? *(page 15)*

How many stomachs does a yak have? *(page 21)*

Why is it harder to breathe the higher you go? *(page 22)*

Index